BLACK AND WHITE

Gilbert Sorrentino

TOTEM PRESS
in association with
CORINTH BOOKS
New York, N. Y.

Love is no comforter, rather a nail in the skull
WILLIAM CARLOS WILLIAMS

For Jesse and Delia

Some of these poems have appeared previously in The Outsider, Yugen, Nomad/New York, The Nation, The Massachusetts Review, Poetry (Chicago), Wild Dog, and Poesia Americana del '900 (Parma).

Library of Congress Catalog No.: 64-22684
Cover by Morton Lucks

TOTEM PRESS
in association with
CORINTH BOOKS INC.
New York 11, New York

THE TRANSCRIPT

I am no tree
no dogwood, nor
red sumac, not
even crabgrass

am a man, a
support but not a
tree, feelings
in me flow in

blood and cartilage.
Do not use me
as flower, bush or
sapling, tree.

THE CHARM

In a dream one sees it.
The touch is there, the taste
is there. The lips press
together, kiss air.

How can this man tell you
what skies hang over him?
How tell you
that you are in the sky

a gentle thing, a tender
thing? How say how much
his fingers hurt for you?
"It is only a dream of the grass

blowing." And that is
so. Only a dream created
by the grass, love bends it
and bends with it, love.

ARS LONGA

Le blanc souci de notre toile
Mallarmé

Carefully as a man tying up tomato plants,
they will to be arranged, the words,
they are all our concern, as that bright
little chainsmoker knew,

what is said is better than said if the
page be impinged upon with power.
Pebbles in a stream, the rings
they cause are unimportant,

the memory of those rings, though,
aha, the remembrance of them the next time
that we hurl the pebbles, there is a
dumb comparison, they argue in the water

as against the water in the brain, the
stream of yesterday's disturbance.   Etched
finely, they neither moan nor weep, the
words, they are neither the experience

nor the telling of it; a barrier of cellophane,
to enmesh you tenderly, or fiercely,
one is here!   one there!   one is in two
or three places at——!   or is it

yesterday, what is this, a poem?
a group of words, a monster of the
evening, it slouches mightily, it is in
full possession of the land and sea,

it fills our sail, it fills our sail,
it fills our sail, it fills
our sail, it fills our
sail, it fills our sail.

THE FICTION

This fire moves.   Upward, upward,
smoke moved by it, forward to the
sky.   I am lost here, where

did we all come from, I listen
to this dear friend's history.
Words batter at me, the wine is

good.   Words beg that I
nod my head, monsters
of the past are here

in the room, a sudden turn and
I will have trapped them.   "What
a time that was."   Here,

here, on my neck: to turn?   God
help me should they have that
face, this face, what face.

SINKING, SWIMMING

She has put her hand
to the door, it swings
open, the sea visible

between her waist and
the crook of the elbow,
shouldering; when he came

nobody's business but his own.
Silence clamped on the room,
he imagines, the sound of wind,

of breakers, the pebbles skitter
among the shells. A
cramped quiet,

water grey between
her waist and arm,
she moves in to the

room.   The door
moves to behind.   The sea
is a snapshot.

AVE ATQUE VALE

We are going away now,
goodbye, goodbye, we are
slowly leaving you, we
are disappearing in eddies

of smoke, the trees are
around us, and I know
you thought we would stay
but we are moving away

now, more swiftly, it
seems.   We.   Who moved
nowhere for so long, that
is a strange animation

there?   It is I and
you, dear, we are leaving
ourselves now, slowly, see
our friends speaking to us

as we depart an inch
or two above the grass, I
can just see you there and I
beside you, goodbye.

IN ARIZONA: DECEMBER

Clouds crawling mountains
the air is red
with dust, the sky

glitters with malice
and pitiful
rabbits are just

about able to keep
their lives whole
in this hell

of tumbleweed
and gasping green
cactus and rock

is the mountains
and rock is the land
and all grace

is distorted there
is no grace to speak
about though

our voices break
contantly into the
stillness

of rock and of dust
and of animal
hopelessness

what is the grace
of a woman whose hands
smoothe her stockings

what is a touch
of those hands on
my face

there is nowhere
to go and to go
is absurd

THE MEETING

1.

We all know too much of loneliness. I used to think
a man came stronger out of it. That might
be so. Testing the old vapidities
is not the same as saying them. They come at you
screaming, they cut up the soul,
injure you remorselessly: these things
that once lay under our surfaces waiting to be used
as objects to cause laughter, are become
fiends, they have northern eyes, blue
eyes, there is nothing at the bottom of them, they
sit in faces that leer obscenely, that take on
the faces, the shapes and declensions of friends. They speak
if you will listen to them, if you can
bear it.

2.

Caelum non animum mutant qui trans mare currunt,
not necessarily so, not at all so, or say that
the sky changes you. I picked up
pieces of petrified wood in Arizona, climbed
a mesa that had stood there 6 million years, it was
made of clay and rose coral, on top of it, I saw
as far as I could see in all directions, nothing: but
sky, but earth, but sky and earth, meeting, the
evil winds laughed at and past me. On the road you sat
in the car, the children in the car, your leg protruded
from the open door, and I was suddenly made barren, suddenly
a terrible aloneness, and the winds
frightened me.
              I thought I should not see you again,
the sky was full of blood and darkness, the blue was
the blue of the west, our west, deadly and implacable, it was
the eye of Satan, of all false gods, the evil eye.

3.

He said he could give up everything
except he could not give up anything
when the test was made of him.   He
is a quiet man, I used to mistake

that for strength
when I was younger.
I mistook it for solidity
and thought all stronger

men were silent.   I have always
talked, too much, and hated
it in myself.   But what is speech
but the release of strength

that threatens to destroy us?
What is speech but
the incantation that can make
men out of mud and mountains

out of slime and nothingness?
"Still waters run deep," is a lie,
bring me the talkers, the windbags,
confessors and liars, the

men who talk all night and all day
who do nothing but talk, who
won't stop even when they have no more
to say, silence

is no more than the lid
of the garbagecan.

4.

I touched you, it was as if
I had never touched anything, you

were water, there was a smell of water
in your hair, your hands
were quick and nervous

fragile to hold and there was water
on them

I want to shatter the winds
that prey on us I reach

through years for your hand.

THE EDGES

My life is too full of faces,
my imagination too full of gestures
full as a garden is of leaves

and colors.   Various movements
in my mind have counterpoint in reality

but I don't want that to be, the gestures
are too much for me.

Sometimes you feel your whole life leaking
out of you as if all your dearest things
were water, don't you find that so?

No one can help you then,
whether you are on the edges or roaring
in the center, your friends seem to be

armed against you and the faces of the drunks
are changed to knives.   The question is

which knives are real?

THE MEMORY

A smell of apricots that brings a place
to mind.   To the eye.   Words twist in the air
in tortured anagrams

shards fall into your life
that once had meaning

you think.   You are arrested and your face
is brought to bear on all of it.   This man

that man.   A woman is in it somewhere
for the asking but the apricots overpower
you, the sentences clamor, voices,
voices.

The air shifts, you thought you were
in the street, you are in a room, what room
can it be, it seems familiar, it is full
of a distant smell, sweet and thin
and these anagrams

are falling into patterns, of course you
are in a room, this is a smell of apricots.

They bring a place
to mind.   These voices are meaningless,
are tortured problems twisting in air.

FACES OF DOOM AND STERILITY

confront him, the dead
faces rising out of the harbor, the mists
that lie on it, move across it with a sigh

moving over the waters.   Confront him.   Anger
him in their acceptance of that thing, that
doom, that sterile universe they inhabit, they sigh

these faces sigh, with soft voices, they are without
anger, wrath, pride or fury, they do nothing, not
well or badly, they do nothing.   They

are blue, what crisp magic they work is to be feared,
it is blue magic, they mutate constantly, one fixes
them with a stare and they are gone, evanescent, moving

quietly over the waters, into the docks and warehouses,
gone across oceans in packing cases, the enemy.   The faces
of misery sing to them but they are in themselves

misery, they seem to nod.   All together, nod,
in agreement and commiseration.   *Misericordia*
but it is not.   It is sterility, guilt lies atop

each of us, an incubus, a succubus, we are afflicted
with Satan, who comes without horns nor in the
shape of the serpent but grinning and full

of understanding for each of us.   As if he would say
what is your problem.   Or did you say
(who spoke?) a Tuesday?   I am here to help you

lying upon you in various guise, mostly a friendly
monster, those faces out there on the waters (that move
on the waters) are my hope and yours.

MAYTIME

So there are the clouds, do not believe them,
pure white or white with blue shadowing
or grey, black, remote, mixed with the smoke
from the stacks of the factory, I ask you
not to believe them, they portend a suavity
which will destroy, girdle a section of city
with a seeming peace and it is really puking
anger.   Do not look at their shapes do not listen to
their shapes, don't think you can "hold them in your
hand."   Nor think they "look like animals."   Nor
initials, nor anything to do with blood, love,
a human warmth.

They are dead

things
      and shape themselves toward death, they are
mist, cold,
freeze the brain
and the soul
emotions die in believing
of them.
Don't go near
them, pull down the windowshade, their hypnotic shifting
will scramble your life, your brains will wither
and crackle, your loves will blow in
dust, borne on cruelty and laughter.   They speak with
the voices of lovers and are lust, they have an odor
of marriage and are lust they are swirling with life
and death hides inside them, do not touch them do not
look at them, they are clouds, sunlight bounces from them
there they are/the clouds/do not believe them.

OUT OF THEIR BUTCHERED HEARTS

They speak to you, give their love
for fearful interest. Look at
the pinfeathers on the windowledge

before accepting it. Or shuffle
the floor, mumble: red? green?
any colorings, turn to

white, request a black.
And one can quietly be seated, speak
of it in a civilized

vein, rather than a sudden
no, or an embracing. Out of their
mad, and butchered hearts

it is held out to you, moon
soft, jagged sun. The white walls
shake their finger smudges at you

take care that you do not
misinterpret them. They are mundane
symbols, and do not prove that

there is anything within you
that should take stock of these
various hearts: merely that people

were here.

THE EVENING NEWS

When you came, it was as if I saw you
through a window, there were people
around you, I caught edges of their shoulders
and arms within the frame.

                            You stood directly
in the center and smiled at me like nothing
ever happened.

My smile was that smeary one
of the deaf and dumb, I offered
a dumb prayer
that bourbon was there,

it is not an out
but it puts you somewhere.

       Through a long winter of snow
and bitter sweepings of the wind I somehow
came through, not with you
but with her, upon whom I at length beamed
that same smeary face.

If there are such things as anger or disgrace
I have not found them here, in anyone I care
for, or in those I love. The calibrations
of these states are smudged so that I cannot tell
if they are fakes or actual precisions.

Anyway it all came out one color and one suit
as perfect as a flush, in spades. The night
drained through the hole the moon had made
and everything was clothed in grey.

BAR GAMES

There was this glittering fuzz
of the quarter as it spun on the bar,
then doubled itself, I spun another,

the glitter cracked into a shimmering fall,
the quarter hit the wall of my glass
the other wore itself out.   I don't care

how much it costs, I am waiting
for you, you are so beautiful it makes him
stagger and he is a queer.   I don't wear

clothes for you but if they are there
so be it.   Let's glut with alcohol
merriment has legs, caterpillars crawl

up, they crawl down trees, my God
the earth, these dazzling quarters
gauge the odor of you.

PAINT

for Dan

What a terrifying
honesty as if someone
should stick his foot
out and trip you
years ago I mean
when the fact that
you didn't cry or
even rub the torn
knee is the fact
that matters, the
honesty of pain which
becomes itself because
our recognition of
it flowers as we seem
not to recognize it.

CARDS

It is black night, spades
and clubs are trumps, hard
to see, the cards on which
their colors agree are

also black.   Some streak
of gulls against this is
what I need, some line drawn
in yellow.   Even blue

would do.   My eyes strain
at peering at this node
of darkness, I wonder why
I could not see it forming,

or question why I did not
question those who could,
as if they knew: they are
obscured as well as the world

in which they move, and
walk.   I hear a voice which
God knows might be mine calling
for a diamond or a heart.

THE CHECKERS PROBLEM

Why does a crowned king
have the privilege of moving

backwards?   To rig a frame
around that, take for instance
Yeats: take for instance

the comicstrips of 1938
that Joel gave me for a birthday

gift.   Some of them have the titles
torn away, though I know the faces
what are their names: Yeats died
that year, now moves backwards,
I demand to know what privilege

that is.   Riding backwards on
those color strips he never
read.   A mystic voice climbs
in the ear, he is riding closer,

he moves in all his privilege,
king, crowned king,
betrayed and dead.   Something like

30 wars between that time and
this offer a suit of guilt to wrap
the self in.   Nothing
to do with Freud and that dull
rationale.   Find me the answer to

that simplest question and why such
magnificence should choose, he, with
the head of Agamemnon, the

bought and muscled back of Lothar
to move in on.

THE MATHEMATICS

He stands before me.   He must be
a friend for his hand
is proffered and his voice, but his head
is a blur
          like they draw speed.

He's hurt me so he must be a friend, that's
the simplest proof in the geometry I practice
which works on the assumption that when one
is stumped one can insert *Identity*.

See, he cries.   That's because he's hurt
me and like a Christian true

and blue, it hurts him to see me hurt
and fumbling with my Q.E.D. improperly.

Maybe in the blur I understand to hold
his head there is a calculus

to demonstrate that the geometry itself
is obsolete and old.

OPEN YOUR MOUTH AND SAY

Ah, how was I to know that the chink through
which I had to go to lay a finger or a tongue
on my own brain was so obscure so hidden so
infinitesimally picayune, I had thought
to do it by the numbers

other methods seemed to me immoral,
ludicrous or fine embarrassment.

The act though proved simply
pain, ah love, I had thought too
that the rain was tied up with the jinx.

It must be kept away!   I hit a door,
my heart doublecrossed me into thinking that
these acts of love were capable of being
shut out, capable of seeming possible

as crossword puzzles.   When will I learn
that abstract love for others puts a six

gun in the hand.   When you cried the chink
gaped and became a wound, I think.

FABLE, WITH ZODIAC

Each thing you thought an
accident
was not.   All ordered
by the slashing

horns of the bull, or the
scuttle of great
Cancer.
What you dismissed

as lightning was a horn
tearing the blue
sky, and thunder
that followed

the lumber of
claws.   A blue blood
dripping from the
firmament, horn

claw and shell
glinting in a rage,
poor things, poor
movers that box

in your life
without
malice, a simple
compulsion to

gash, crawl, your
history born
without your or
their knowledge.

THE ABSTRACTION

The shape of the gesture,
the form of it before
it entered the blood
was silent, silently
it moved through the air

quiet enough for him
to figure its movement,
describe it to himself
while the blood
waited.   His predictions

externally true, he was
tricked upon entry, it
turned to a color!   He
could not see it, his
blood swirled around

and about it, but the
touch told him nothing
but black.   Was it black
in the air, was it black
in the gesture it danced

in the air when he looked
at it silently moving in
air as it moved toward
the blood in a form made
of silence, and turned

to a color!   A color
of blood which is black
as it moves as it feeds
the black brain and black
heart we all give a color.

DOMINOES

It's too obscure, it's as it were
a slab of pie a glass of icy milk
in summertime, that's what he thinks
she's brought to him

though I think differently.
What I think is a link in a chain
of rain that goes from April
to September, how wet the ground

gets! What you think is in
the shapes that chortle in your latest
paintings, you can't hide them
they are referential of you

but there he is too.   There is pain
that is black and that brown stands for
pain, the bitter red strains to encompass
pain, my word

it has become our definition or
our shadowing, the sun won't even come
in country windows anymore, the city long
has swept itself toward black

the total is as if one might
walk in that say, August rain, to a barn
and see a father there
swinging in thin air.

TWO FOR FRANZ KLINE

1. THE GUNNER

The color of a pass
is
        black and white, so is

the color of the world, break
our heads and make our voices

hoarse as we will
in denying it.

        Black and white,
        7 and 11

hell is black and heaven
white, the models
for the world we live in.

Birds fly, beetles fly,
birds and beetles borne on
thin winds lacking color, borne
miles to obscure ends, without

an argument the fact is
held and so accepted, black

and white, life
and death, eggs and dung
and procreation and the life

goes out in tiny heaps of dust: where
        color is is
        in those places we
        have made within the

world, but they are
simply, places, the world passes
        hugely on each side, huge
        and black, and
        white

2. THE DARK HALLWAY

Love is not involved, a black
and white world.   White
dresses move
                    across the black

waters of the lake.

Are dimmed as night comes down, they
move too, in ignorance of love, love
is not involved.   Black and white,

simple,
        a throw,
                movement, and over

there the grass is green as the
ladies see it, lie upon it, move

over it, but to me it is black
                        grass

nor even grass, black
masses, clumps of black

upon which the ladies' dresses
are still, and now I hear

their voices, far, a natural thing
without colors, tones or shades, natural

voices.

THEME AND VARIATIONS

Find a wind in the mind
before which each kind
of lined face will erase
its own disgrace.

    A wind that has picked
on brains and flesh and decay,
    swollen over the sea, grown
thin and switched to acid

    on the plains. Dumb,
wind that keens and tears
    its belly out on mountains
hurls to the other sea

    and puts out the pain
in that moiling tapestry
    of foam and crisscross
slashings. A wind.

    Moaning of his voice, groaning
of her voice, I strive toward
    understanding them, I translate
wrongly, and the moan, the groan

    continue. I commit
the sin of gilding the poor lilies
    that they grow from those
effusions, wrongly, wrong.

    Take them out of the boxes
they are in, place them in new
    combinations, nothing good
comes of it, they are pigeon

    holed, nothing good can
come of it, they fly off into
    the wind, caught
in a suicidal wind, whipped to

find a wind.   In the mind.
Before which each kind of lined
face will erase
its own disgrace.

THE LANGUAGE BARRIER

There is a movement.   Is it
a word that moves against
the air, the ear.   It

is my own word I recognize
although the tones it encloses
are less strident than they were

in certain times of stress.   It
moves with the flaw of the dance:
exists for myself alone, the

flaw of dancing measures and
explains it.   I do not even know
this word, yet it moves in the

air toward my ear.   Those who
might understand it are blind
to the motion.   It should turn

with the fury of rats in a
trap, gnaw itself free of the
prison of space I have placed

it in.   This prison it dances
in, dumb to the world, has
made it a thing with no

sound of its own, not real
to itself, not true to even
its stupid directions.

WHAT I MEAN IS

Great blocks of sunlight describing
.the boundaries of love, what are
these boundaries? Where are these
boundaries ending, great shapes
of sunlight fall on the paintings,

the room is white, the rooms are
white, the leaves turn as the year
goes out. In a dream of color
the year shifts subtly to fall.

The fall is a dream, in Duncan's
beautiful phrase, of the grass
blowing—that is a secret and
the telling is secret, a whisper

wrapped within whisper, a question
at the end of it, to tantalize.

This, I swear to you, is secret,
I don't know the answer, you don't
know the answer, it exists in the
shapes of sunlight that wake us, I

have seen blown grass, heard it
also, run on the beach with the
sound of my own despair in my ears,
yet loved the grass, the knifing
wind attacking it. Now you and
I are within that dream and the

fall is around us, the boundaries
of love are unknown, they are what
we wish to make of them, see, they
run to the edge of the windows
and fall out, splintered, each

fragment holding love and suddenly
lost in the enormous sun that covers
the brilliant world it dreams.

AS WITH A SIMPLE GESTURE OF THE FINGERS

three lives hung on two.   A motioning
of fingers

and two rushed together.   The rest
a construct, how high!   how impossible
to see the top of it, it took so long
to make!   And with the pointing of a finger
and two fingers, a swift line drawn in
air that lingers only in the lover's eye,

and all the bricks and spirings be dust,
be rubble.   I move my fingers, their
mechanics are familiar, where have I seen
such motioning before?   and your fingers
are familiar to me too.   Don't be proud,
I fight that imposition of my heart, this

is such a small outbuilding now, such
embarrassment to live in it, the dust
and relics heaped about, not yet moved away.

As with a simple gesturing of fingers
all my words are turned to singer's words,
held and polished for your unique delight.

THE LONG GOODBYE

All night I spent turning
my head over my shoulder, turning
back toward those things that when they
happened I turned from, in a dodging

of pain, how well I avoided what
should have cut me, spilled, at least,
blood. I remembered my
voice, the texture of it

a weaving of shadows, the light
before thunderstorm. I am happy,
I said (the voice flashed its light),
happy. Sun in the garden.

The garden's movement in wind was
a palimpsest upon which your movement
also recorded—and I saw only the green of
the leaves, the ripening beans, the

tomatoes. You moved away in the sunlight.
Turning back over my shoulder, turning on
my back, my side, I cried into the dark
and she answered. Now God will me

and help me to feel all the pain
I must feel to become all the man that
I wish to become, and to make my voice
into a record of love with no turning.

THE BARE TREE

It appears that each bare branch of this
sorry tree holds swaying a face

of me, the wind commands them in their
movement, the childish face that life

once gave to me is clear and perfect,
the exact old photographs my mother

took of me, what a stranger there
bending in the wind, changing

to someone just a little more like
I am now.

I give you those old visages, the clothes
too, time has thrown into its bag

and love along with them and along with that
whatever face I hold up to you now

and vow this face is honest, fragmented
only by the changes love forced into it.

COUNTERPARTS

A lover's moon behind his eye
or a moon for maniacs, cringing
there, passion and utter lunacy
stagger past it, one may say

they are the clouds.
What kind of thing pain is
made of is discoverable there,
the ragged paring of the moon

holds that complication. What
textures, colors, maddening
abstractions that spill together
to make pain this is

solvable. And the moon cringes
lest a moon in some strange lover's
eye, or madman's eye, seize upon
it, drawn by the glitter of despair.

WHO GOES THERE?

The vicious tight curl
of the pubic hair in the
bathtub, or a mass of black:

birds measuring the limbs
of a tree, these box in
a world full of demons

who are arrayed in black
in back of the world made
manifest in lusterless

porcelain, brass pipes
turned black and greasy
green, God damn those

nervous birds, the demons
possess them! They sway
—how long is that limb,

what grinning face inhabits
the friable leaf that
determines its tip—?

Someone, prove to me what
tender strategy will over-
whelm it, scrub it all

bright with the silvery
cables of bridges, tides
of love without logic

cracking the brittle
shapes the demons inform, forms
burned clean in a gout of flame.

THEME FOR PAINTERS

They have to have each other,
don't ask me why or is it some
obsession to dirty up the world
that pits a hard, a bony shoulder
dead against their softest
bellies—
        death keens in winds
out of the north, out of

the east

Brother Rat

I'd break it open if I knew
the formula, without it it's all
a friendly greeting in the

evening time, heaping plates of
meat and gravy with a side

of bread
        but the wind carries
on outside, it punches at these
windows old
          Brother

Rat—but such an "open face"—

older, older, what wisdom that we
come to merely measures

off our years, our grey hairs
spell out scum of wisdom, O

the endless heart
is broken

—endless wind in the
rigging of—what bridge
              is that—?

THE SHADOW KNOWS

A flowerpot the color of earth
in Maryland: into which
birds look, turn from, look
again,
        fly.

It is empty, full of
air only
        that has come from

—Maryland? or Canada,
perhaps

it's cold enough for that. Mixed
with the air is there

another colorless substance
from 10 years ago, call it

the past? Rust-colored
is simpler to say, but

not so precise as that
color of Maryland earth

rain makes it moreso
the color, and so does
the earth more

become as the flowerpot

though birds stay upon that

Who heard
        what birds, and

shrieking of wind past
the butterfly windows . . .

        in my mind this
        very flowerpot
        its very angle.

THE BRIEFING

Or, listening to subtle lights
of the vowels
pinched

out of the dark letters
that stagger around
and about

and die

away. Break with
an axe, into it

now, free them for
the kids in the
park, even for

the mealy-mouthed
bastards who never
cared

and won't ever
care . . . lady,
silent vowel of

a woman, broad
or flattened, open
(as all vowels are
open), pressed against

the hard phallus
of—
      b, c, d, you

have your instructions, now

move out!

SHAPES OF WINTER

1.

To believe in a world of beauty: O
says the moon.   The screech of the
birds answering the belief, the interjection
of the moon.   A world of beauty,

silv'ry moon behind all of it, the light
turns to measure the crying
of birds, their crying inches toward
light, when they mesh, what

will occur?   What world of beauty
occur, those black daubings spattered
on the moon revolve around

a stately ugliness, churn, settle.
Flight.   My eye reflects a simple

bird-like movement, dumb hanging
world, lost in its bitterness of white, a
sad man's face hacked out of it.

A smashed kite in a tree
its stars are bleeding
down on the grey coats and faces
moving beneath, let them
turn up their faces
and welcome it, the blood, do they

know that it's death?   Let them turn up
their faces themselves, I can't, where are those
that rave
                    in a professional tone?

This collage on the door,
made out of busted newspaper, and its
stripes are bleeding down
on me.   I don't know that it's death

it is simply, there.
                              What tokens
of love our crude hands
fashion, and break.   Broken love,
bleeding in stars, bleeding in
stripes, blacks/whites, and

the red/white/blue of our
bunting.
                    Grey faces, muddled races
look at the dripping of death and

see in it love, so humbly fashioned
and so broken by our
fumbling hands.

3.

Shall I have it
pretty? Add a lake to it,

say that it shimmers, that
it glimmers. The sunlight
skids across it on the
wind. I'll have it pretty

or know the reason
wry. Birds hop among their
own droppings (strike that, I'll
make it pretty): among the

shafts of buttered sun
that la de da.

Here, "and here," is a piece
of orange glass, orange, yellow,
spectrum mellow, O the winter
settles in, I'll have it

by the hair, the razored edges
of the orange glass shall cut it
for me,
          in this shallow season
          I shall know the reason

why: to render it all up and
make it pretty, ah, this tarnished Shiva

glares at me—

4.

Grey settles
down, pearl lights
sway against the branches

that the wind
should sway

and out there ·is
love, soaked by
wind covered
in loneliness

but she knows

that love is not
grey and hangs to
the pearl gleam

of the lights that light
the park, the trees
they turn to marble

mocking spring and
all that saccharine
of green, that blast

of color, green for
envy, or the monster
whose head is truly

frightening, but each one
knows, a sight to look upon
or else our hearts may

stiffen to the marble
trees that should sway
in these auguries

of snow, that stand in
this scarred season, O
that stand so

5.

The edges of these buildings cut
the edges of the air and I
take what gloom upon myself?—

one year now since softer
weather, we all remember that
gentle temperature, Christmas
bells ringing through persistent

warmth.   A miracle!   A birth,
a virgin birth, ah, old friends,
their faces split in two with
merriment above their egg

nogs!   A miracle!   The edges of those
buildings blurred in sloppy
air, a miracle!   How hot is it
in the Congo, you say a cold

front's moving in?   What gloom
I take upon myself, 12 months of
brand-new life for me, the virgin
birth, a miracle!   The edges of

these buildings frame the snow.

6.

The night of the first snow
a polar bear lumbered between us!

the snow was white against his
whiteness!   and your eyes
were dark, ah!   winter

wonderland, this stringent
city!

(DIRTY GLASSES)

The delicate lacework of the fire escape
ends abruptly at the top and bottom of each rail
in whorls that remind me of eyes behind
spectacles that look out upon a wet and frozen
world.   In whorls that hold in their centers
a delicate lacework of trees that remind me
of nothing but trees that are cold and depleted.
One black and rusted lace laid carefully upon
a brown and sodden lace is the true shape
of winter that I know.   If I were to stand
in the park—what an amazing idea!—the lace
of the trees would lie upon the black and the rust
of the fire escape, the whorls would be whorls
and wouldn't remind me of eyes.   Who sat in
the room that I wouldn't be in would contemplate
a wet and frozen world (seen through the window)

SILENCES

Out of a quiet mood of night
come women's voices, so far
away that they are the white
figures at the other side
of that dark lake in the picture
that hung in my hall as a
child. Now that I think
of it I know that they
were not people but sails
perhaps? Or rays of light
the painter squeezed through
leaves of the giant trees,
but in my mind they must remain
people, lost in the swift
evening that bludgeoned them
and drove them to the little
light remaining in the shimmer
remaining on water, and what
were they speaking of, and
what were their names, and now
though I hear their voices in
the night all I can tell for
sure is that they are women's
voices, soft and white, wrapped
in white vowels floating above
the white gowns that cover
their limbs, lost in the rushing
darkness of the summer evening.

EMPTY ROOMS

the constant is vision
                    —Olson

What we see is really there,
whether it be there
or not, or a heaped image
of the mind, the focus brings it

to reality: we see.   Then
what is the shape of love?
Or what is its color? Is it really there,
to be conquered, to be maintained
in a shudder of exertion? What eyes

does it look from into ours, does
it exist
          in the place it has lately been?

It leaves
a skinny, bewildered
perfume, that is its

terror, that and the
fact
of the odor, the pitiful

sound of old laughter.
                    We are cursed

in the need to stare
at it, break it open to
reality, turn the shifting
and hapless thing that it is

into a picture of some old
emotion: a beach, a fire, hot
summer nights, what

was the name of the person we
talked with? And the curse is squared

as we invent, make real, it is
real, we will it so.

THE LEGEND

In this great field, terror
takes the shape
of emptiness: there

is the sun, a blue
veil over it, with
white sparkles sprinkled

over that, they are
stars, it is night
now.   The sun is

empty, a huge zero—
and a figure with head
averted stands

against the blue
clot shining hope-
lessly.   There will

be no more dawns.
For him.   For
whom?   The figure

stoops, he is looking
for the beans that
hold his mother's

head, his father's head.
He is the dead part
of the mind, stricken so

when that ignorant
woman walked between him
and the part that lives:

who also stoops in a
field, blue, dull sun-
light, head averted,

nothing to be heard
but sighs and breathings
of the grass.

THE DREAM, SQUARED

A figure, a door, the door as you

is you. The woman
that has so long

stood inside of you will not

go out, the one outside as equally beloved
will not come in. Dreams,

dreams, the immobility of dreams.

* * *

Whose blood is it they drink
to find a speech to tell
me that they don't wish
anything to happen that
isn't happening? Whose

blood do they drink to find
speech; roulette, the black,
number, the red number, what
is my number, spinning
voices to tell me have found

speech to tell me

WHAT SHAPES HIDE

for Philip Guston

there, behind the harsh
colors?
        There, a grinning
face, a twisted body, the tyranny

the hunchback in the mind
imposes. What shapes

that elbow in the black smears
separating colors?

I have come to the city and
the city is a room, all rooms
that have been lived in, a-
lone, there are shapes

in every room, that is a city:
all cities welded, wedded to

these interminably leering
faces, these broken bodies

heavy with ether, clouded with
colors, they find their

easiest freedom in the
twists they suffer in the twists
of black.

A DETAIL

Where earth is, is also
water
     is not true of necessity.

Although where earth is, water
may be, poured on by a hand
holding a can
          or glass, or maybe

rain?
    From this we may infer, if
we be mad, or look into ourselves
crookedly: where love is, is also

those things which cause love—though
this is neither more or less true

than the paradigm above (of necessity). What

we come to know is that the wind blows
and the sun burns, legs take you places
if placed one before the other regularly.

There are other things, too, we know them
just as surely, but about

love, and water, earth and all simple things,
it is enough to find them out

simply, singly, make no mistake
about rules, it is possible to forget

even your children's voices.

CORINTH BOOKS Modern Writers and Poets

LeROI JONES, The Moderns: An Anthology of New Writing in America. Cloth, $5.95

THE BEAT SCENE, an anthology with photographs by Fred McDarrah, edited by E. Wilentz. $1.95

MODERN POETRY FROM SPAIN AND LATIN AMERICA, translated by Nan Braymer and Lillian Lowenfels. $1.45

DIANE DI PRIMA, Dinners and Nightmares. Stories and poems. $1.25

GWENDOLYN MacEWEN, Julian the Magician. A novel. Cloth, $3.95

DAVID OSSMAN, The Sullen Art. Interviews with modern American poets. $1.45

DELMORE SCHWARTZ, Successful Love and Other Stories. A collection of new stories written since 1950. Cloth, $4.50. Paperbound, $1.95

In association with **TOTEM PRESS/LeROI JONES:**

EDWARD DORN, Hands up! $1.25

ALLEN GINSBERG, Empty Mirror: Early Poems. $1.25

LeROI JONES, Preface to a Twenty Volume Suicide Note . . . $1.25

JACK KEROUAC, The Scripture of Golden Eternity. 95¢

FRANK O'HARA, Second Avenue. 95¢

JOEL OPPENHEIMER, The Love Bit and other poems. $1.25

GARY SNYDER, Myths & Texts. $1.25

GILBERT SORRENTINO, Black and White. $1.25

PHILIP WHALEN, Like I say. $1.25

FOUR YOUNG LADY POETS: Carol Berge, Barbara Moraff, Rochelle Owens, Diane Wakoski. $1.25

In association with
JARGON BOOKS/JONATHAN WILLIAMS:
BOB BROWN, 1450-1950. $1.50

CHARLES OLSON, The Maximus Poems. $2.50

LOUIS ZUKOFSKY, A Test of Poetry. $1.75